In the
Temperate Zone

In the Temperate Zone

Poems by
Judith Kroll

Charles Scribner's Sons : New York

for my Mother and Father

Contents

I

State Of The Mind Address

I pull out my hair
like doll hair
as if I could always buy more

and the loose flesh
the thighs

could always be tightened
by a string

but now I am busy
with other things

a clogged head
little red eyes

keeping things in and down

denying
all the things I have
and must now own

Dick & Jane

Dick is the one with the weenie
who gets to be doctor
and never cries,
in love with mechanics and motion.

Jane is the one with nothing under her skirt,
so soft and weepy,
in love with the rulers of earth.

Dick gulps his soup and burns his tongue.
Jane blows and blows to cool hers,
it takes so long
she has ages to see

that Dick is just a boy
with a rubber jiggler.
She can take his tongue on hers and cool it off.
She can cut off his thing at the root.
She can tuck him in bed and sing him to sleep.
She can leave him alone.

Dorothy

I'm melting! melting! O what a world,
what a world! Who would have thought
a good little girl like you
could destroy my beautiful wickedness!

The Wicked Witch of the West

Later I knew
it was never a dream,
but a glimpse;
a prevision
of life.
Only in a real world
do things have color,
get born either
Good or Evil
and you never know why.
And then I followed
the difficult bright road
to the dying city of tricks.
Nothing was magical,
the flying monkeys were not magical
if you knew
what their true names were.
I saw
my senses unseam me,

I could die of a flower.
I was the spotless quester,
whose innocence affronts.
I did the task
too hard to do,
and watered the Witch
who dissolved like sugar.
I went again
to my master's throne
only then to discover
that nothing is unexplainable.
The old man flew.
I closed my eyes upon a wish,
falling back into death.
Something indestructible
clamped my heart.   The ruby shoes
turned into flesh.

A Poem for Priscilla

for Priscilla P. St. George

Dressed up tight
in her best clothes to go;

a son, a divorce,
a book written
sad and strange
as her own west wind; spectacular
unhappiness.

Wonder who pulled down the shades,
and how she ever noticed it.

It's cold in the world
with no man on.

They tried to burn
the dark excesses out.
Last spring,
picnicking with friends,
imperfectly remembering
what books and things
were needed for doing

you never knew what.

In the kitchen,
unheard,
electricity hums.
It is a little like the world
which has always evaded hands,
yet is everywhere, the ultimate love,
if you will step in water
and touch.

In Memoriam
Autumn, 1968

Who To Look Out For

A man who thinks women
are always undressed
in the mind of God,

one breast held out,
a handful of grain,
an offering, a feast—

and one foot forward,
the hips at a slant,
and hair that never gets dirty,

a mind like a broken trap.

The mind of God
is clear, pure;
the air
is the air above the timberline,
where things are transformed
if they would survive.
Nothing frivolous happens here,

no matter how it might look.
All is present,
yet distant,
the loudest sound
happening to someone else
on a neighboring mountain.

Into this
walks Woman—a bagful of gimmicks—
says the professor,

says the professor, with a knife
in his eyes
and a crotchful of pain,

on his knees,
begging for it.

Dead Teenage Girls

Dead teenage girls
line the streets of heaven
waving their boyfriends' rings.
Someone important is coming.

Not Jimmy Dean.
Not Lenny Bruce.
Not even Bobby Kennedy.

It is someone whose name will terrify you.

When I was sixty-two

When I was sixty-two inches tall,
I lost my virginity to someone
six inches long
               (everything
seems larger in memory)

says Debbie Reynolds.

If you look real close,
you can see
that her face is merely a glacier,
covered with flesh-colored moss.

Ages and ages ago   she too
had ancestors   stirring the fire
honestly killing.
              We have come
to this (This bit goes over great
at parties)

she says, her small tears making
mountain-streams.

The Secretary

The secretary takes
a pencil from
her bun of hair,
a yellow pencil,
number 2.
The secretary smiles,
the smile breaks
on shores of her having removed
the pencil from her hair.
The boss
is brown-suited.
He smiles at her
he smiles
at how her breast
moves out at him,
a question in the curve
of her upraised arm.
He thinks it is an inquiry.
The secretary
is not thinking at all.
They have fully

misunderstood, their lives
turn on a thing
that has never taken place.
They become lovers
and husbands and wives
and small and old.
All over the house
there is nothing that is yellow.
One day he notices and mentions it.
She says, either:
Look harder
        or
Make of it what you will.

Watching "Chief Crazy Horse" on *The Late Show*

I

Trink Barton,
Harvard lawyer; Linda
Darnell, late of
Southern C., meet
in a forest, meet
beneath a mountain,
and then she getteth her
upon her knee, open
her mouth, let her tongue
tell him history.

II
An American Myth

There was a scene
that afternoon—the sun
was a hot brown
on the things
you had to say.
A desert lined my eye,
I shed my snakeskin.
What can I say,
our frontier is nearly
ended, the cities
are loving themselves
like gods, but
                behold,
something comes
to save the day,
the reel jerks hard, and men
pour into view, they are
shouting something,
they are shouting
Gold! Gold!

III

Believe me, the Great Leader in Washington
wants none of your sons to die
he will protect them, they fight
for their own good

                  sandy
creek, the red deer, autumn
in the small pool

                  Now perhaps
there is something you'd care to say,
confidential? Relax.   They will think
we just drink firewater together; there's
nobody here but us jews.

Imaginary Guns With Real Bullets:
An American Dream

I like any story
as long as it ends in blood.

When I kill them in my dream,
I walk to the A & P
and line them up against the dairy case.
There they stand,
sealed off by glass,
mouthing the words that stick to them like burrs.
Their motions are ludicrous,
underwater divers sensing
something going wrong.

I think of my father, the noise he made eating.
I think of my mother, but not her name.

I am so full of love I can scarcely take aim.

Week of June 5th, 1968

The nun in the bathroom
washes her hands
as if she were not a nun.

Inside a store
a jigsaw puzzle
of Marilyn Monroe
is together to show
how it looks when it's done.

The nun has a skin
that has aged in a vacuum.
But her eyes are trapped
exotic birds,
they are like the eyes
of Marilyn's face,
the cardboard sarcophagus.
Everything
is twice-removed.

This time,

the funeral games
on television
purge not sadness,
but belief.

It has used itself up.

No one has died.
No one ever will.
Life is a liquid
which takes the shape it has to.

Then the dark box clicks
out the sound of trees.
And there are
no trees.

The Man Who's Against Everything
Appears on T.V.

What kind of house is his mind like?
It would have a stuffed
deer-head
on the living-room wall.
And a deer-head
in the hallway, by the door.
And one in the basement, near the bar.
And three in the bedroom
of his three small children:
baby deer for baby children.

Science Fiction Poem

The palms of their hands were mirrors.

And in their eyes
vipers curled, the tail a point of light,
two green pupils beaming out their rays.

And if you unbutton their shirts,
part the cloth aside,
like opening a triptych, you will see
the pit of agony, lusts, and deaths,
a maggoty pie.

And all this while they stand completely still,
permitting it,
not even looking passive, resentful, or dumb;
simply permitting it, knowing where
and why the power lies.

Trees

I thought if I thought of dying,
then that would make me safe.

But I should have seen before
that this was the wrong kind of spell,
like burying fish
to make things grow.
I thought it did the opposite.

The train bumps
over tracks,
invisible bodies.   Trees
hold blood
instead of sap.
Don't cut.   We
are trees.
              Spare

Woodman
has locked his door,

and bought a gun.

He reads his Bible every night.

Violence will come
to those who prepare for it.

"Open in the name of the President!":
a poem for Mr. Nixon

He sits:
a bonnet framing his head,
the wings of a shawl clasped over his chest,
a smile on his baby-face—
knitting names into a sweater.

The memory bank
already knows the worst.
The names it feeds on
do not give it indigestion.
If it could grin,
it would grin.
If it could be someone
it would wear a sabre,
gold braid, and shiny leather,

whose power swells and flexes
and grows wings;

a golden bird, an aztec god,
it floats

over the seas

and roosts at the back of the President's chair.

It gently folds its wings across his chest.
The President smiles and smiles.
He hugs himself, he feels so good.
He does not know that anything is there.

1970

Trip

for Alfred Chester, 1928–1971

Why didn't you take a taxi into the interior?

Deeper, deeper,
where the lushness of things is an extra dimension.
Exquisite, inscrutable taste,
and everything clicks and fits like a plastic puzzle.

You could love yourself there.
Your hands passing over your body
are blessed.
You could ask yourself: Why didn't I have
this dream before?

Wasted time—
hanging in the air,
settles like dew on the fat leaves
of the rainforest.

You could have stayed,
wandered there—the animals so mute and good

and whatever you do to yourself means nothing to them.

One day you would have toppled like a tree
aged one, two hundred years,

looking young, without a wrinkle on your face,
no lines in your forehead,
because nothing ever bothered you,
and no one ever told you about death.

Poem about Death

You can't have too many
poems about death.

No sir.

You can't have too many poems. Why I

remember once
when I was a boy   my horse

broke his leg,
and I had to shoot him.

Bird of Paradise

There was a pretty
word I heard once.   Its name,
I think, was azalea.   I must have
known it from my other life,
when I was the hawaiian princess
who to save the land from something
which must have been evil jumped
naked into the volcano under
a veil of flowers

Me Jane

Me Jane.
Me write poems.

You wiped your glasses,
and permitted yourself a smile:
If I've told you once
I've told you twice,
I will not put up
with that kind of behavior
at certain times.

I said Growl Growl.

You took off your belt
for a whip; your bare boots sank

in the green rug; from somewhere
a smell of lions
arrived; lead skies,

heat, flies, a kind of hay.

I pounced.
You fought your best.

After awhile
I did not know what I was after.

About the Author

When it was the latest year,
a year like 1860, say,

they sat,
ate meals,
and thought: I can't believe
that this is it.

They worried about death,
they put it off,
and finally they could put it off no longer

and the children who stood
crying, crying, at open graves,
were thinking of themselves,

their future, already over,
already the unknown selves
who would fill their shoes
crying at some future parent's death,
already using it as
something to get over,

a theory, however fractured,

however much nothing fit,

to blur things, make them easier,
leave things behind,

they stood,
they cried

unchanging tears.

Two Poems

I
The Brain Theory

        There is a theory
of the brain
that says
      um . . um . .

It is your theory, you have made it up;
I have made you up,
I make up
the things you say, I create
your laughter at these very words.

Now that I've painted myself
into this corner,
I will relax
with a can of beer.
The paint fumes ripple
like desert air.   Later
I will think of what to do.

II
It almost rained all day

It was the heavy kind of day
in which your mind feels coated,
like a tongue.
What are these gestures
I drag along,
black snakes
on a black plain?

If I do
not pay attention,
I will write the same poem
again and again.
Perhaps I've already done it.
I am that dim.
If you take a minute,
you will convince me of it,
whoever you may be.

The turpentine rises from the floor
like flowers.   I did not foresee
this end.

Natalie Morningstar

lounged in the teeth
of the afternoon,
white scarf tied around her hair,
tennis-virgin
in the recreation room.
Eyes dark fava-beans
cut and dyed and shaped to look
like eyes.   The music moves,
a liquid meadow
on a painted screen.   The summer air
breathes fast: *you will have lost,*
you will have lost.

In a different kind of real world
a girl suffered
and heart grew flat, because she loved but
could not sleep with him
no matter how well he played the piano,
she could not.   Her background laughed.

And once at least in a car

after the drive-in and the painted screen,
she made me what I am, saying
Take my brown beauty,
I am a teenager,
my life moves in scenes.

A Tree Grows In Israel
(revenge, pity & fear)

Three trees.   I paid for them,
gave my money to the U.J.A.
three different years.

One ought to be fifteen or so by now,
waving its arms
like a teenage ballerina
drunk with adolescence

the stain on the skirt

cannot be hid.
You can try to hide it with your hand—
Renée and Dottie will find you out,
walk by and sneer:
Girlie you got
red ink on your pad.
That ain't no blood.

Their huge breasts badge them with power.
Mine would lie quiet in an undershirt.
They know things,

I smell it.
They do things with boys.

And ahead in the postage-stamp future, they stand,
their husbands the hardhats of catholics and jews,

who would believe
they ever loved boys

their hair in curlers
their make-up on
their nails are done
they push their carts
their mouths snap shut,

turtles whose cases last on
though the meat inside dies
and melts into smells;
their bodies will litter the suburbs
with hard green shells.

I think of Housman who said the poem
is a morbid secretion, like the pearl

You are the grain
of sand in my side.
I cover you over
with layers and layers
of papery pearl.   Poems,
there are hundreds,
microscope-thin.

Their ink is all invisible, is not
the important part as each
addition wraps around.
It has got so big
I cannot hear
my heart through the mountain.
The grain is far away,
like a childhood myth,
the good angel
who changes dimes for teeth.

Where does it all come from?

Doctor,

what does it mean to have
a white stone of considerable size
growing beneath one's
skin?

I see.

Two Doctors

Once in a dream I saw
my mother in his chair,
the doctor on the couch,
curved and naked as an embryo,
his head on my chest,
my hand on his silky hair.
It was very difficult.   Mother,
I kept saying,
he's *supposed* to be asleep.   But still
she had her doubts.

In the dream I haven't had
I go to a doctor
out of the blue, I say
Doctor, everyone is
a 6-foot flower
in a huge field, and I
am a tiny bee; don't speak
the language; am ineffectual.   You,

for example, are becoming
a puffy dandelion.
                    And he,
opening his yellow mouth, will say:
I think that's very beautiful;
I'd like to write it in my little book.

Surprised, I smile.   A *friendly* flower.
Safely I buzz in and between
his velvet surfaces,
and feed: "I don't mind that you're going
milky and sour.   You're a hell
of a nice weed."   He says:
blow me away.

Bed

The lights are off.
Across the room
it sweats
out of the walls,

its breath warms up
like a cold motor.   I lie
and watch its body
thicken and swarm: I am
as irresistible as food.

This must be a dream,
or else I am falling asleep.

It moves.

Unbelievable,
like really seeing
a wine-dark sea.

It has no mouth.   It says:

You fooled around enough.   Flirted
and tempted.   Jeered.   No one
can pull my leg: I

am the daddy whose name
is death, and come
to tuck you in

& in
& in

The Shadow

our "negative identity" haunts us at night
                                    Erik Erikson

Give me what I need!
She's there across the street from me:
confident, young,
graced with a beautiful walk,
a faceful of luck.
No one would ever notice that we look alike.

I shuttle from doorway to doorway,
in love with her life:
it's all a red carpet,
it's easy, it's safe.
Rejection, when it happens,
seems almost her choice,
she shrugs it off so well.
Why doesn't it work for me?

I pull my collar close, careful to stay unseen.
Look at that posture!   Straight as a queen,
she turns each imperfection to a jewel,
makes each flaw interesting,

like they tell you in magazines.

My heart collapses, a weight,
a dead star sucking itself.
I swallow the daily poison in my throat.

I don't want to be on the outside looking in.
It should be so easy, the right kind of plan,
a matter of possession by surprise—

I'll wait until she sleeps, then go to sleep,
and wake up in her eyes.

The Penn Central Makes Some Connections

Everyone is nodding on the train.
The passengers are almost asleep.

The midday sun shines straight into my eyes.

It is the air,
hot and sedative,
that fuzzes our brains.
What the train breathes out,
we are breathing in.
We realize our sleepiness
is not from lack of sleep.

Everyone
is annoyed;
a sense of community grows.
I am the one
chosen to find the conductor
who has gone to the tip of the car.
I rise and balance down the aisle.
                                        I smile
upon each passenger, one by one,

furry and white,
sheep after sheep.
The end seems so far.

No wonder the water is so still.

The river is sealed
by a skin of oil.   The shore, edged

with rainbows, is alive with
unnatural color.

The train goes by a bridge;
blocks of metal,
grey stones stained,
and the water slimy, black.
Smokestacks,
wrecked cars, nameless factories,
tractors, cranes,
incriminate the shores.
In the middle, in the thin
water-lane,
a college crew team practices.
Their colored hats are almost invisible.

As they lean forward and back, they are

pulling away
from sickness, but getting weaker
with every stroke.

The feathers of the birds are dull.
ALL kinds of litter, trapped
in trapped currents,
moves up and down
as in a dream,

the dream in which I kill a girl,
for some reason,
with a knife.
No one knows I've done it,
except me: and that
should count for something.

The police have come to take her away.
I happen to be the one
to point them to her room,
not knowing who she is
or where I am; not having seen
her face.

For the funeral they blow her up again,

like a balloon.
Her cuts have been sewn;
her skin is plump and smooth
and stretched to bursting.
I cry like a relative all the way home.

I think this is some kind of school,
but I know nothing else.

I make up a list of clues:

The grass is unnaturally green.
The sky is sealed.
The air is dead.   I am alive

only because I don't

breathe.

Familiar

No, it isn't a butterfly,

it's the death of my father
which hasn't happened yet,
a gaudy blot,

a blind cancer
flying to the center of my heart—

the gyroscope that ought to keep things steady,
good with the bad, deaths past and coming;

but it wobbles wildly, a crippled top,
and the child writhing beside it,

a man moving away,
the knife under his coat, hot with baby blood,

and the little girl, me, lying mortally wounded,
knowing she will get up and die on for sixty years
after that man in the coat:
it was my father.

Sign Language

i.   Punch & Judy

Up front
in the auditorium
the puppets
batter each other and howl;

one croons again and again
the sinister refrain
I feel
I feel
I feel
like a morning star

It is a poem inviting doom.

The puppets cackle and scream.
I am, for the first time,
afraid in a way that is new;

something springs alive,
a kind of fear digs in

that will last as long as I do.
The quality
of this apprehension
will not

be dimmed by time
or be refined

or in any way changed.

ii.

I liked you better in the old days.
In fact
I liked me better in the old days.

The old days
when things were younger
(I might have said *greener*
in the old days)

A summer night:

the possibility

of infinite joy—thinking it was only
a matter of time.
                    Kissing by a lake:
eternal kisses, the cinematic sky,
the moss, the pulsing air;   later
the nights were never like this,
each star in place, the sky
displaying all its wonders,
like a planetarium.

iii.

A summer in camp:
I am the most popular girl.
It never happened before,
it never happened since.

Being left-handed
paid off in sports—it always had
in my mythology—

Fifteen: captain of all the teams,
best runner,
forward, guard,
batter, server,—and

good-looking,
even though not a blonde.
I deserved the power I had.

And the world
so beautifully heightened: things

so wonderful because I
was wonderful

iv.

says a famous ghost.
Say about a thousand voices.

Again and again and again
the morning stars

v.

The I in this poem is not me.
This is not meant in a trivial way,

as it is of a photograph.

Even if it were possible,
I would not wish to be entirely on the line.

vi.

Hearts bleed
from discernible causes,

leaves peel
off forearms, expose
the leaves beneath.

Out in the Gobi desert, things are hot.

Words
are really something
else.

That bleeding
has got to be stopped.

Some people

are so *American*.

A mirage—

I feel I ought to know you from somewhere.

vii.

The flash-bulb blinds me.

In a pool of light
in front of a window, I stand

in a Mexican dress:
fat white cotton,
embroidered in blue and red.

I am five,
my fist full of peanuts
the photographer gave me
to keep me in my pose.

Hold out, and you'll get what you want.

I operate by this truth,

though it fails more often than not.

viii.

At the end of life
I don't know what to find.

Who can believe
that all it does
is go from beginning to end,

transforming ignorance
into knowledge
or intuition
or a guess.

The terror has a source,
this old, incurable fear:
I feel
the heavy truth grow inside me
like a star.

Once it was dark,
then it bruised to red,

soon it will turn to ash,

a whisper of butterfly dust,
a whisper in somebody's ear;

or denser and faster,
a collapsing face
too heavy to let out light—
a sucked-in hole in the mask of space.

*In America a psychologist couple . . . have taught a
young chimpanzee the sign language of deaf-mutes . . .
This chimpanzee has really succeeded in understanding
syntactic language.   She makes up new sentences.
For example, she says things like*:   "You, you and I,
together, let's go into the woods."

On the Farm in July

The horizon slows down from its spin,
the air comes to rest like a snowfall stopping.
An incandescent scene, the full circle of it,
a miniature painting of gods:

each bird, each tree, and each flower
outlined and bright, infused
with its own clear light; they do not need the sun
to light them up, the sun is only
a fiery disc in the sky,
caught up in a fever of inwardness.

The flowers, the trees on the hill,
the long waves of grass,
brighten and sharpen.
The silence grows to a sound.

The moment prints into your cells, you think;
and yet you forget it and live in a dream
till the next time,
if there is a next time.

Above the Weather

Up here
the sun is always shining

and white clouds glow,
whale-sized,
in an endless ocean.

Only the generous clouds
the distilled blue air
and the sun in meditation,
as blank as it looks,

here at the center
the same calm sun

smiling forever into its border
which endlessly extends.

Let the jungle be your guide

follow it
into the green blanket of heat,
tiger-bright flowers choking your pores.

The bees of the jungle
are larger than anywhere else,
the size of cannonballs,
the heads of fabled men,
myth replacing their history
atom by atom.

Each bird is an eye
that nothing can blind.
Turquoise and gold,
they ride on the tops of trees
that are denser than mountains.

Now, in the evening,
winds split on the walls
of your skull, a small temple.

Its people
are open and tranquil as air.

The sound of their bells
is the only sound that you hear.

II

Not Thinking of America

Floating across the lake,
lotus-pads upturned with the blank look of clover,

the sun, an unseen presence behind a curtain of heat,
intensifies every tree and flower,
urging them forward like talented children;

the sharp charcoal smoke of the boatman's hookah
floats back in waves, enters the dream,

romance and violence.   On the other side of the lake
Shalimar Garden waits;
water-channels, marble pavilions.

Down on the plains, in the winter palace,
a courtier might have been flung from a tower,
the hands of a child cut off to teach a small lesson,

one among many in a realmful of bodies—
playthings, a scattering of coins;
and the wall of blood forever waiting to burst,
an unseen presence, wherever the eyes are turned.

At Shalimar things could seem different,

the pastel valley a landscape of rest
for minds too tired to rest by themselves.

She never existed, one woman the cause of it all;
there might have been someone exquisite who almost
        deserved it,
but she would have been a point of departure,
the small occasion for a larger dream,
who could not really be trusted, though she took on

a luminous presence when set like a pearl in the
        garden,
the garden set in a valley,
the valley an emerald
set in a ring of mountains, a hard cold ring.

Akbar's Tomb

Approach through the great stone gates.
Twilight of a humid, overcast day.
The grey breathless sky illumines the sandstone tomb,
the dull red color soaked into a huge bare plaza,
quiet desert of stone
in a heaven of generous spaces.

Crowning the tomb, clusters of cupolas, level on level,
a mountain made out of open spaces,
domes so light they seem anchored by slender pillars,
as they tug always upward
in a yearning for oneness.

And now the muezzin's mosquito-whine voice
unreels from his tower.
It moves for miles over fields, and courtyards, and
      trees.

What did that flat, high whine say to Akbar's ears
as he sat in his palace
drinking his mixture of opium, wine, and spices,
examining miniatures painted with brushes of three
      fine hairs,
debating with Jesuit priests, concealing the date of his
      birthday?

How did it sound to the French ambassador

who has given up yearning for France?
The heat, by its sheer persistence, has taught him
    something.
His silks and brocades sag as he walks in a garden,
the thick grey sky
sinks his heart like a stone.

Alone, in the cow-dust hour, he walks by a formal
    lake—
dull, still, shut by the heat.
The moon-white pavilion in the center
sends its glow to his bones.

He no longer thinks of France, of anything.
His eyes let in the sky.

Before he turns back for the evening meal
he feeds himself to the air, the trees, the fishes,
he cannot help it,
he is filled with invulnerable joy.

A Walk in India

1969, 1972

The lawn lies bright and cool,
the sky soaks up my thoughts—
they have gone to another dimension
to which I have no key.
There is nothing to do but to rise,
go out the gate, walk down the dusty road
to the fields of the marigold farm
where flowers are growing for garlands,
for weddings, for the altars of gods.

Flocks of parrots, baby green,
wheel and swoop, stealing the marigolds,
making off with the fat gold heads.
They must taste strong and nutty, a dessert.

I wear the sari I wore three years ago
walking in the orchard in Kashmir
where plums and apples crowded the trees
and cannabis grew everywhere—
under the branches, along the paths;
the village men sat on blankets, sorting fruit,
passing a hookah and singing hymns.
They looked up and smiled through ivory teeth

as I passed to the fields beyond
where women tending crops
wore thick silver anklets and bracelets, their whole
    trousseau.
I took my time, I didn't mind being
an event to date things from, a special treat.
At the evening meal they told the others at home
all about the texture of my skin,
the thinness of my hair,
the bangles on my arms.

And it seems I'm still walking back then.
That scene continuing, matching me step for step,
each gesture perfect, superimposed,

I walk through the marigold farm
on the raised dirt path between the flower beds
and the two scenes merge, squeeze out the years
    between,
that spongy filler, the strained drugged days in
    America,
layers of bad static, never enough time.

From a place I cannot name
I watch myself now, tomorrow, it happens forever—
I am walking here in the future,
my waist is thick, my hair is grey,
a mole on my nose holds a bead of sweat.
In the dulling sun I move through the fields

more than half in a dream,
wondering where it all went, and why it seems
I never did anything.
The women squatting at work look up as I pass,
their eyes full of mischief and questions.
They see that it's safe, that I'm not a man,
they can stare as much as they like.
They take in my clothes, the color of my eyes.
In high light voices they ask each other
where I am from, who is my husband,
if I have children, grandchildren,
and who will get my jewelry when I die.

The Missionary Spirit

I'm beginning to understand it,
mother of meddling thought.

These teasing associations—

how Buddha's father, a king,
was told his son would renounce the throne
and go out in the world to solve the suffering of men.

The father determined to cancel this fate
and rescue his son from not being a king.
He built him a paradise: all the prince saw
was innocent and good,
beautiful and young.

But one day, from his chariot, he saw an old man;
the next day, one sick;
and then one dead.
Three awful hallucinations!
The thunderbolt struck, he learned it would happen
     to him.

His innocence so extreme,
it couldn't have stunned him more if his father had
     planned it.
Age, illness, death, bore down with a force

that could have turned coal to diamonds.

He had to become Buddha, or else go mad.

And also this: the well-meaning prince,
riding along on his big white horse,
pierces the terrible forest of thorns
with an idiot grin on his face.

He's about to rescue the princess whose father the king
had tried to protect her from spinning-wheels,
but nevertheless she has slept for a hundred years.

The prince approaches the end of his quest,
the frozen scene
with the ruby lips at the center.
A happy end.

But the story sounds deeper,
more ancient than that—
its true meaning lost or shriveled away,
leaving only the narrative bones.

It could have been a lesson that goes like this:

The spindle-prick of the finger was the moment of
     light.
The curse that brought it was the unasked gift of
     grace.
The one who arranged it all was the self that everyone
     shares.
The princess was the soul.
The prince was the ignorant world.

And I think of the women in purdah, my female
     relations,
set deep in their intricate households, their husbands'
     jewels,
but jewels of magic and power.

What should I do, as I chew on my paan-leaf politely,
pull out some curse from another dimension—
"Sisters, you know
in America people would say you are slaves?"

We can't say much, we sit and smile,
our faces warm the dimming air.
Their eight young daughters, five to fifteen,
all stand around, a shy, pretty chorus,
staring and staring, and all but one
refusing to speak a word in any language.

We chew more paan-leaf, each green pouch

fat with tobacco and cardamom, pinned with a clove.
Our tea mugs steam and sweat on a silver tray.

They have sent for the bangle-woman to come from
    the market.
She arrives, swathed in white: nothing shows.
The enormous bundle on top of her head
is full of glass bangles, in shiny snake-coils,
dozens of colors, patterned and clear.

My sisters-in-law, fifteen years older than me,
giggle like girls: it's unlucky for me to go barearmed,
I must choose.

We all confer with each other; the girls cannot wait
to point out the bangles they want, and have them
    wrapped up.

Sounds float over the courtyard wall,
crows and parrots settling for the night—

more tea is coming.   I sit, and watch,
and hear the sound of wind-chimes on my arms.

Somewhere Else

The villagers blur in the distance, and the sounds
    of cows,
already almost home.

The end of daylight, the sun a lamp
in a darkening room.
The wet earth changes its friendliness for a chill.

I sit here nevertheless,
close to the river's edge, screened by weeds.
Grasses and trees weave around me in a web, framing
    a view—

the river spreads out of sight, off the side of each eye,
as it should,
a long bandage smoothing my brow.

The sun's yolk bleeds into the sea, somewhere else;
for me it bleeds into the river, a grey satin mirror
framed by black banks.

The heaviness of the hour
blurs my outlines into air.
The past shrinks in the distance, out of sight.

Let the tiny figures gesture and shout—

my parents, my sister, my husband, me.
It doesn't bother me.   It doesn't matter
any more than a stranger's album.

My mind is clear
and fit to think these things.

If I could sit here forever—if I could still be sitting
     here
even when I leave,
I think I would be all right.

Ram Ganga,
India
January, 1972

In the Temperate Zone

(New York, New Delhi)

Night is so tiny here,
the sky a few inches across,
a small planetarium dome.

The moon rises: a mercury bead
sucked up in the chill night air.

Heat and light have fled to the other side—

there a marauding sun
blinds the blue sky of India,
the sky spreading over the fields, out of control,
there is so much more than is needed.
It even undoes the image of America,
dispersing it into a pitiful sprinkling of rain
that falls inches apart and is lost in the dust,

dispelling years of the worst predictions come true;
the invisible plague that turns everyday people to trolls,
blind eyes bulging with meanness, with cheapening
     hatreds.

There it goes, the breakable toy,
the game that even the rich can't afford to play.

Nothing seems alien here.
The landscape stuns by its lack of pretension;
the wiry tangles of mesquite that always remind you
    of something
litter the roads and fields where nothing else grows.
Primary colors glow on village women
under the sky that is always nostalgic or brutal.
Moist hot winds, descending, drag along
exciting storm-clouds, the weird illumination.

All over the countryside things conspire
to reassure you that you are nothing.
You don't even have to try to believe it.
You don't even have to pose under the stars.
It hides in insects and eyes and in withered grass.
It hides in children teasing the peanut-vendor
who squats and patiently fans his charcoal fire.

The sky, smeared pink and grey, and the failing light
bestow uncertainty, a sense of illusion.
Evening thickens, giving birth to sounds—

only the sounds are firm and clear;

the temple bells and chants, the call to prayer,
the hollow notes of cows with their mindless eyes.
Parrots neon-green in the shimmering air
whir into the village to roost in the trees.
A baby's cry

blends with the noise of goats and cows
and people talking, as they travel home,
walking, or riding, along the canal.

Quick birds skim like gnats on the clouded water.
The canal runs eighty miles, it goes all the way to Agra.

Sestina

Is this the object:
not to let things pass
without noticing,
without being in control,
at least of a clear sight?
There are so many things worth nothing.

I sit hour after hour, doing nothing—
dreaming of India, a far green object,
a blinding sun hung on the edge of my sight.
One moment I think I am writing, the next I pass
into infinite fields, and a sky whose control
rains absolute, unnoticing.

I try to think—but find myself noticing
each word sealed off from its thought by a round
        nothing.
Something is out of control;
I do not even object,
unaware that the hours pass,
that the present moment is buried from sight

by this vision of me in India, allowing my sight
to filter off in the distance, noticing

my feet pass over the lawn, my eyes pass
over and over the garden, settling on nothing.
Such a relief, sight without object.
Such a relief, to let control

be a process like breathing; to let control
lie in the targets of sight,
lie, if anywhere, lost in the heart of the object,
and to let the effort of noticing
soak like rain in that tree, that flower, that nothing.
Every moment something is coming to pass.

I remember a high brown mountain: a pass
cut through it, jagged, holding in control
the animals, trees, underbrush, and sky—nothing
escaped, not even my sight;
and the pass extinguished itself at a temple on top,
      without noticing
it had used itself up, it had reached its object.

Is this the object: to pass,
without noticing, beyond control,
beyond fixed sight, beyond nothing?